Heart of a Servant

A Daily Journal

"...you have left your first love."

Revelation 2:4 (NKJV)

Dr. C.

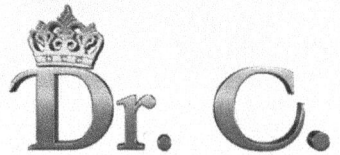

clfpublishing.org
909.315.3161

Copyright © 2025 by Cassundra White-Elliott.

All rights reserved. No portion of this book may be reproduced, stored in a retrieval system, or transmitted by any form or any means electronically, photocopied, recorded, or any other except for brief quotations in printed reviews, without the prior permission of the publisher.

Cover design by Senir Design. Contact info: info@senirdesign.com

ISBN #979-8-9925784-3-0

Purpose of the *Heart of a Servant* Journal

Our lives can become very cumbersome with our overcrowded schedules filled with commitments, family gatherings, social events, and personal ambitions. Even as followers of Christ, we can become distracted away from the Word of God and our covenant with Him.

This 30-day journal provides one scripture per day that will remind you to return your heart to the Lord.

After reading the scripture, journal what comes to your heart and mind. Spend time reflecting on your love for God and His love for you. Taking just a few minutes each day will remind you of the genuine love you have for Him.

Date: _____

> *"Love the Lord your God with all your heart and with all your soul and with all your mind and with all your strength."*
> **Mark 12:30 (NIV)**

Personal Reflection

_____
_____
_____
_____
_____
_____
_____
_____
_____
_____
_____
_____

Date: _____

> *"We love because he first loved us."*
> **I John 4:19 (NIV)**

Personal Reflection

_____
_____
_____
_____
_____
_____
_____
_____
_____
_____
_____
_____
_____

Date: _____

"Love the Lord your God with all your heart and with all your soul and with all your strength."
Deuteronomy 6:5 (NIV)

Personal Reflection

_____
_____
_____
_____
_____
_____
_____
_____
_____
_____
_____

Date: _____

> *"Know therefore that the L*ORD* your God is God; he is the faithful God, keeping his covenant of love to a thousand generations of those who love him and keep his commandments."*
> **Deuteronomy 7:9 (NIV)**

Personal Reflection

_____
_____
_____
_____
_____
_____
_____
_____
_____
_____
_____
_____

Date: _____

> *"Love the LORD your God and keep his requirements, his decrees, his laws and his commands always."*
> **Deuteronomy 11:1 (NIV)**

Personal Reflection

_____
_____
_____
_____
_____
_____
_____
_____
_____
_____
_____
_____
_____

Date: _____

*"... The LORD your God is
testing you to find out whether
you love him with all your heart
and with all your soul."*
Deuteronomy 13:3 (NIV)

Personal Reflection

_____
_____
_____
_____
_____
_____
_____
_____
_____
_____
_____
_____

Date: _____

> *"But be very careful to keep the commandment ... the LORD gave you: to love the LORD your God, to walk in obedience to him, to keep his commands, to hold fast to him and to serve him with all your heart and with all your soul."*
> **Joshua 22:5 (NIV)**

Personal Reflection

_____
_____
_____
_____
_____
_____
_____
_____
_____
_____
_____
_____

Date: _____

"Love the Lord, all his faithful people! The Lord preserves those who are true to him, but the proud he pays back in full."
Psalm 31:23 (NIV)

Personal Reflection

_____
_____
_____
_____
_____
_____
_____
_____
_____
_____
_____
_____
_____

Date: _____

"Let those who love the LORD hate evil, for he guards the lives of his faithful ones and delivers them from the hand of the wicked."
Psalm 97:10 (NIV)

Personal Reflection

_____
_____
_____
_____
_____
_____
_____
_____
_____
_____
_____
_____

Date: _____

> *"I love the LORD, for he heard my voice; he heard my cry for mercy."*
> **Psalm 116:1 (NIV)**

Personal Reflection

_____
_____
_____
_____
_____
_____
_____
_____
_____
_____
_____
_____

Date: _____

"Jesus replied: "'Love the Lord your God with all your heart and with all your soul and with all your mind.' This is the first and greatest commandment."
Matthew 22:37-38 (NIV)

Personal Reflection

_____
_____
_____
_____
_____
_____
_____
_____
_____
_____
_____
_____

Date: _____

> *"To love him with all your heart, with all your understanding and with all your strength, and to love your neighbor as yourself is more important than all burnt offerings and sacrifices."*
> **Mark 12:33 (NIV)**

Personal Reflection

_____
_____
_____
_____
_____
_____
_____
_____
_____
_____
_____
_____

Date: _____

> *"Woe to you Pharisees, because you give God a tenth of your mint, rue and all other kinds of garden herbs, but you neglect justice and the love of God."*
> **Luke 11:42 (NIV)**

Personal Reflection

_____
_____
_____
_____
_____
_____
_____
_____
_____
_____
_____

Date: _____

"And we know that in all things God works for the good of those who love him, who have been called according to his purpose."
Romans 8:28 (NIV)

Personal Reflection

_____
_____
_____
_____
_____
_____
_____
_____
_____
_____
_____
_____
_____

Date: _____

> *"But whoever loves God is known by God."*
> **I Corinthians 8:3 (NIV)**

Personal Reflection

_____
_____
_____
_____
_____
_____
_____
_____
_____
_____
_____
_____

Date: _____

> *"May the Lord direct your hearts into God's love and Christ's perseverance."*
> **II Thessalonians 3:5 (NIV)**

Personal Reflection

_____
_____
_____
_____
_____
_____
_____
_____
_____
_____
_____

Date: _____

"God is not unjust; he will not forget your work and the love you have shown him as you have helped his people and continue to help them."
Hebrews 6:10 (NIV)

Personal Reflection

_____
_____
_____
_____
_____
_____
_____
_____
_____
_____
_____
_____

Date: _____

"Listen, ... Has not God chosen those who are poor in the eyes of the world to be rich in faith and to inherit the kingdom he promised those who love him?"
James 2:5 (NIV)

Personal Reflection

_____
_____
_____
_____
_____
_____
_____
_____
_____
_____
_____
_____

Date: _____

> *"But if anyone obeys his word, love for God is truly made complete in them. This is how we know we are in him."*
> **I John 2:5 (NIV)**

Personal Reflection

_____
_____
_____
_____
_____
_____
_____
_____
_____
_____
_____
_____

Date: _____

"Do not love the world or anything in the world. If anyone loves the world, love for the Father is not in them."
I John 2:15 (NIV)

Personal Reflection

_____
_____
_____
_____
_____
_____
_____
_____
_____
_____
_____
_____
_____

Date: _____

> *"If anyone has material possessions and sees a brother or sister in need but has no pity on them, how can the love of God be in that person?"*
> **I John 3:17 (NIV)**

Personal Reflection

_____
_____
_____
_____
_____
_____
_____
_____
_____
_____
_____

Date: _____

> *"This is love: not that we loved God, but that he loved us and sent his Son as an atoning sacrifice for our sins."*
> **I John 4:10 (NIV)**

Personal Reflection

_____
_____
_____
_____
_____
_____
_____
_____
_____
_____
_____
_____

Date: _____

> *"This is how love is made complete among us so that we will have confidence on the day of judgment: In this world we are like Jesus."*
> **I John 4:17 (NIV)**

Personal Reflection

_____
_____
_____
_____
_____
_____
_____
_____
_____
_____
_____
_____
_____

Date: _____

> *"Whoever claims to love God yet hates a brother or sister is a liar. For whoever does not love their brother and sister, whom they have seen, cannot love God, whom they have not seen."*
> **I John 4:20 (NIV)**

Personal Reflection

_____
_____
_____
_____
_____
_____
_____
_____
_____
_____
_____

Date: _____

> *"In fact, this is love for God: to keep his commands. And his commands are not burdensome."*
> **I John 5:3 (NIV)**

Personal Reflection

_____
_____
_____
_____
_____
_____
_____
_____
_____
_____
_____
_____

Date: _____

"...keep yourselves in God's love as you wait for the mercy of our Lord Jesus Christ to bring you to eternal life."
Jude 21 (NIV)

Personal Reflection

_____
_____
_____
_____
_____
_____
_____
_____
_____
_____
_____
_____

Date: _____

> *"Above all, love each other deeply, because love covers over a multitude of sins."*
> **I Peter 4:8 (NIV)**

Personal Reflection

_____
_____
_____
_____
_____
_____
_____
_____
_____
_____

Date: _____

> *"I have been crucified with Christ and I no longer live, but Christ lives in me. The life I now live in the body, I live by faith in the Son of God, who loved me and gave himself for me."*
> **Galatians 2:20 (NIV)**

Personal Reflection

_____
_____
_____
_____
_____
_____
_____
_____
_____
_____
_____
_____
_____

Date: _____

> *"For God so loved the world that he gave his one and only Son, that whoever believes in him shall not perish but have eternal life."*
> **John 3:16 (NIV)**

Personal Reflection

_____
_____
_____
_____
_____
_____
_____
_____
_____
_____
_____
_____

Date: _____

> *"Greater love has no one than this: to lay down one's life for one's friends."*
> **John 15:13 (NIV)**

Personal Reflection

_____
_____
_____
_____
_____
_____
_____
_____
_____
_____
_____
_____